Rose
B
Imp
Politicians

CW00530076

Martin Rosenbaum is a writer and journalist who worked for many years as an executive producer and producer in the BBC's political programmes department at Westminster. He edited Radio 4 strands such as *The Week in Westminster* and *Political Thinking with Nick Robinson*, and produced documentaries on topics ranging from the inside story of Gordon Brown's premiership to the politics of *The Simpsons*. This is his first book of satirical verse.

Rosenbaum's Book of Impractical Politicians

A poetic pastiche

Martin
Rosenbaum

Copyright © Martin Rosenbaum 2021
www.rosenbaum.org.uk

The right of Martin Rosenbaum to be identified as author of this
work has been asserted by him in accordance with the Copyright,
Designs and Patents Act 1988

All rights reserved

ISBN 978-1-7398005-0-5

Published by Rhododendron Publishing
www.rhododendronpublishing.co.uk

First published in 2021

Cover illustration & design by Simon Ellinas
www.caricatures.org.uk

A satirical pastiche and parody
of the poems in *Old Possum's Book of Practical Cats*, by TS Eliot,
applied to the world of contemporary politics

With my acknowledgements to Old Possum,
il miglior fabbro

To Chloe and Hurley,
our impractical and practical cats,
and the rest of the family

CONTENTS

BORIS: THE PRIME MINISTER

There's a shout in Number 10 at 11.27,
When the crisis team's ready to take part,
Saying "Boris, where is Boris, is he somewhere reading Horace?
We must find him so that Cobra can soon start!"
Carrie, Wilf and Dilyn, and anyone who's willin',
They are searching Downing Street,
Saying "Boris, where is Boris, sometimes he's slower than a loris!"
But it's urgent, so now Cobra has to meet.
At 11.57 the decisions have been taken;
The officials are now frantic, all alike.
Then Boris will appear, his mood is full of cheer,
He's been riding around Stratford on his bike!

    He ruffles the top of his bright blonde hair,
        He mentions his great-grandad was a Turk,
    He mumbles some words such as 'um' and 'err',
        And everybody else gets to work.

People say that by and large there is nobody in charge
Of the team at Number Ten.
So the spads and all the staff, and the cabinet's top half,
They jostle for position now and then.
Boris likes to take a nap, if in meetings there's a gap;
His mind wanders when his interest isn't piqued;
For he's not a 'girly swot', unlike Cameron and that lot,
As he wrote upon a memo which was leaked.
He may go out for a jog, or he sometimes walks the dog,
And he's pictured as he scurries round the park
By a snapper on his team in the government machine,
While ignoring missives from the duty clerk.

You can have no hope that he'll relent;
His habits can't be made to go.
So nothing's aligned in government
When BoJo's running the show.

Getting Brexit Done was his purpose number one,
And it helped him win a triumph at the poll.
He's always cracking jokes that can entertain the folks;
That sometimes seems to be his leading role.
He likes to go on trips, where he makes his merry quips.
He does visits round the land and some abroad.
If disease is on the rise, then to medical surprise,
He shakes hands with all the patients in the ward.
He's often making schemes to construct his latest dreams -
An airport or a tunnel or a bridge.
But his plans meet lots of traps when he wakes up from his naps
(The oven-ready deal's in the fridge).

And so we muse about his strange career,
Him going all the way to Number Ten:
It raises the chance, it has to be stated,
Of being an olive, when reincarnated,
Since this Bullingdon boy, then full of joy,
Was chosen the nation's PM!

The new family of Boris have to live above his office;
Carrie doesn't like the decor that she sees.
Around the rooms she fusses while he's painting model buses,
Or he's gazing at his bust of Pericles.
If he's stuck up in mid-air, say a zipwire got him there,
He wobbles and he waves his little flags.
He wants to be a booster, not a gloomster or a doomster,
Even when his hopes are hitting many snags.

Yet ever since at school he has wanted so to rule,
With his key ideological trait -
It led him to fame, it's the aim of his game:
To eat his cake - AND have it on his plate.

So he pines for a role he still hopes to become,
    As youthful ambition has stirred:
If the ball was to come, loose again, from the scrum -
    The king of the whole wide world!

THE KEIR STARMER WAY

So he's the Labour leader now, his name is Sir Keir Starmer;
It's often said he needs more vim, since he's not one for drama.
As politics is raging on, he seems to stay above the fray;
He waits and waits and waits and waits -
    for that's what makes the Starmer way.

    But even though waiting's his tactic of choice,
    He now and then thinks of ideas he might voice.
    He likes to make his broadcasts by a flag of large extent,
    So the public sees that he's a patriotic gent.
    He'll also pose for pictures in a big department store,
    Hoping that with voters it's a way to build rapport.
    A lawyer from north London, he has to be discreet -
    The group he can't be seen with is the urbanite elite.

So he's the Labour leader now, his name is Sir Keir Starmer;
At PMQs his questions are as dry as Atacama.
He calls for tougher measures that were coming anyway;
He waits and waits and waits and waits -
    for that's what makes the Starmer way.

    But given that waiting's his tactic of choice,
    He takes lots of care on positions to voice.
    He got to be elected on a unity campaign,
    So if an issue's tricky then he's happy to abstain.
    He once was a Remainer, but that's all in the past;
    Europe can't be mentioned - the thought leaves him aghast.
    When young he was a member of a group of Pabloites,
    But now we're not sure where to find the Starmer acolytes.

So he's the Labour leader still, his name is Sir Keir Starmer;
For now he won't have policies that could provoke bad karma.
If he brims with manly passion, then it's for another day;
He waits and waits and waits and waits -
   for that's what makes the Starmer way.

    But noting that waiting's his tactic of choice,
    He tries to forget his most lawyerly voice.
    Knighted as the DPP, he doesn't like the 'Sir';
    It isn't quite in keeping with the socialist milieu.
    And he was once a barrister who helped fight Maccy D's;
    Now he's pictured dressing smartly, not in tracky b's.
    He makes his points quite softly, in muffled monotones;
    Could he have been desired by the solo Bridget Jones?!?

If Starmer gets to Number 10, all this will seem most classy;
If not, perhaps the dream lives on that he could be Mark Darcy.

DOMINIC CUMMINGS: THE STRATEGY MAN

Dom Cummings thinks up brilliant plans, they call them 'Classic
    Dom',
For he's the master strategist who fights officialdom.
And he delivered Brexit, yet soon found he was to spare,
But if you look for who's at fault, then *Cummings wasn't there!*

So Dominic, yes, Dominic, there's no one quite like Dominic.
The weirdos who he hired thought that he's a weirder maverick.
He says the current government just drives him to despair,
But when you search for who's to blame - well, *Cummings wasn't
    there!*
He wasn't in the Cobra room; in Sage, an empty chair;
He'll tell you once and once again, yes, *Cummings wasn't there!*

Now Dominic's a clever chap, that's what he likes to spin.
He wore a hoodie at his work, without his shirt tucked in;
His brow is deeply lined with thought, his head shaped like a dome;
To state his case he always quotes an esoteric tome.
He says the rest make errors as they think within a group,
But he can break outside that as he knows the OODA loop.

So Dominic, yes, Dominic, there's no one quite like Dominic.
The idiots in government, they could not grasp his top logic.
His office was in Downing Street, he walked through Parly Square,
But then his views were overruled, like *Cummings wasn't there!*

He's greatly intellectual and reads all the smartest nerds;
He blogs his thoughts concisely - in say twenty thousand words.
He likes to drive long journeys, though it's said his eyes aren't
    good;
He made a trip in lockdown but, alas, misunderstood.
How best to check his eyesight and the glasses he should wear?
Well, visit Barnard Castle - and so *Cummings was seen there!*

If a minister was subject to bad briefing in the press,
Or a chatty rat was leaking and yet no one did confess,
There may be a WhatsApp message but it wasn't in his name.
'Twas pointless to investigate, our Dom was not to blame!
And when some spin was published in the papers of the day,
"It must have come from Dominic!" is what the pundits say;
But Dom was surely not the source defaming Carrie's dog,
As his time's spent reading Bismarck and amending his old blog.

So Dominic, yes, Dominic, there's no one quite like Dominic.
He sought to run the beating heart of Britain's body politic.
And he was once the hero of a drama put on air,
But now today where power lies, DOM CUMMINGS ISN'T
    THERE!
A dodgy slogan on a bus, a top electioneer,
Or will he find his legacy's a psychopath's career?
Yet if the chance comes up once more, he could ... take back
    control,
And if there is a sequel they'll give Cumberbatch the role.

MR RISHI SUNAK

Perhaps you know Mr Rishi Sunak's
Most magical tree made of money?
When the economy's right down the dunny,
And he's not very keen on a new tax,
And the upturn hadn't begun, he
Had to raid it for all he could get -
Though it rather increases the debt.
So 'whatever it takes' he would do,
Whether or not it's true blue.
   His swelling reputation
     For being brainier,
   Helped to sweep across the nation
     A Rishimania.
The greatest magicians have something to learn
From Chancellor Sunak's major U-turn.
Manifesto?
   That has to go.
     And we all said: OH!
      Well I never!
     Was there ever
     So fertile an endeavour
       As Rishi's most magical money tree!

To be a Jedi was once his ambition,
And he wished to be strong with the force;
But now he's switched over his mission -
To promoting 'Brand Rishi', of course.
Thus he poses while wearing a hoodie
For photos at work at his desk;
He's not washy-wishy, in fact he's quite dishy;
And some say he's most statuesque.
   Now Rishi's the man in the frame
     In ads his team often tweet out,

Ones that are signed with his name -
Like when we were told to eat out.
So the brand recognition's most good,
For the man with the fashionable hood.
And we all said: OH!
Well I never!
Did you ever
Know someone so eager
As Rishi, the Richmond MP!

Coca Cola's the drink of his dreams -
Mexican coke is the best in his views;
And he's snapped making tea for his teams,
Supplying them Yorkshire's best brews;
But he's not at all one for the booze.
He drinks coffee however, it seems,
From a cup that's elite, in maintaining its heat;
And he's often on diet regimes.
From head boy and then PPE,
To banker and safe Tory seat;
And he's maybe the richest MP;
But still there's one goal to complete:
Though he never picked up his lightsaber,
Will he fight out his Downing Street neighbour?
And we all say: OH!
Well I never!
Was there ever
A dapper frontbencher
Like Rishi, the man and the brand!

GOVE: THE NIGHTCLUB MAN

Gove is the chap who had had quite enough
Of experts who always are wrong about stuff;
And as for the ones who think they know best,
He said that the British are far from impressed;
And somehow this leads to the strongest of whims
When the groups of the experts possess acronyms.
But Govey himself is not a young pup.
Right now he's the minister levelling up.
Of other jobs too, he's been an amasser;
Recently, Chancellor, Duchy of Lancaster.
Food and environment once were his scenes;
That was the time when he charmed all the Greens.
And when the Lord Chancellor, Gove undertook
To give inmates more access to reading a book.
Being Chief Whip was a role he had too,
Though he missed a key vote, getting stuck in the loo.
A witty debater, who often outsmarts,
He has played in his time many possible parts.
But still he looks back on his happiest job,
In charge of the schools and defying the Blob.

He once was at home in the Notting Hill set,
That came to an end when on Brexit he bet,
And Cameron was cross that he couldn't depend
On someone he'd seen as a trustworthy friend -
A feeling that Boris was later to share,
When Govey dropped out, with just hours to spare,
Of backing for Johnson as leader to be,
He'd suddenly thought of a new nominee -
A man to surpass all the others who strove
To be party leader, a chap surnamed Gove!
A stab in the back, or a stab in the front?
One can't use the term that his enemies grunt.

But his proudest achievement, his most favoured job,
Is still running schools and berating the Blob.

He's also a fan of the show Game of Thrones;
If he's found in a garden, about it he drones.
And really his hero is Tyrion Lannister -
A figure reviled, yet strong-willed in character.
Here's doubtless a fact which for some will appal:
Vladimir Lenin's displayed on Gove's wall.
You can't make an omelette without breaking eggs!
To get through his programme, Gove had to block Clegg's.
With some of the views that he chose to assert,
He mailed them out in the name 'Mrs Blurt';
One of these emails simply said
        "AAAAAARGGGGGHHHH!!!!!!", a
Sentiment fitting the whole of that saga.
But as Govey looks back on his choice of career,
Maybe it's time for a different idea:
While noting his impact on practice and rules
When taunting the Blob and controlling the schools,
Some think there's a bigger achievement, perchance
(Whatever one's view of his policy stance) -
        That moment of mystery
        When he made history
In Aberdeen's nightclubs, as lord of the dance.

JACOB REES-MOGG: MAN ABOUT TOWN

Jacob Rees-Mogg is not like a hog,
In fact, he has little spare weight.
This physique sprawled out shows, in his leisurely pose
When bored by a Commons debate.
And he won't have substitutes for the double-breasted suits
That always envelope his frame;
As few rabble-rousers have such well-cut trousers
In which nanny has sewn one's name.
The tasty foods he begs are Cadbury's creme eggs;
He brews cider he likes to consume,
In amounts that he meters, in pints not in litres -
For metrication just causes him gloom.

The son anachronistic of a father nicknamed 'Mystic
Mogg', Jacob is himself a parent of six kids -
The latest is called Sixtus. They live out in the sticks, plus
A house in London town worth many quids.
Brought up by a nanny, he soon became quite canny,
Investing in the markets from age 10.
Eton-educated, with habits quite outdated,
He insists he'll only use a fountain pen.
He drives around his seat in a Bentley from his fleet;
He's conscious of one's status, low to higher;
And so his staff he schools, in etiquette-based rules:
Only men without a title are 'esquire'.
And he's very happy that he's never changed a nappy;
He isn't what you'd call a modern guy.
He's often said to be the honourable MP
For a century that's passed and said goodbye.

Some people like to scoff, they say he's such a toff,
But he also has his many devotees.

A feature of his tribe is a patriotic vibe;
They think fish are more serene in British seas.
Unfailingly polite, this figure on the right,
His Jacobite rebellions are no more.
Once dubbed a 'pushy fresher', he has to face the pressure,
And Moggmentum can't keep going evermore.
He used to filibuster - long speeches lacking lustre -
As a rebel with his own distinctive slants;
Now he's Lord President, inside the government -
Like he said, we can't be run by potted plants!

ALEX SALMOND AND NICOLA STURGEON

Alex Salmond and Nicola Sturgeon were a closely associated
    couple of Scots.
As mentor and protégé, leader and deputy, working together on
    SNP plots,
They had an extensive reputation. They fought their case together
    in a manner energetic;
They wanted Scotland's oil, and a border overland right from
    Gretna through to Berwick.
They put it to the people, who responded with a 'No', from
    Shetland down to Ayr;
She's since become the boss, and their old collaboration's now a
    feud extraordinaire.

    If with staff there'd been a 'sleepy cuddle',
    And this had been with alcohol befuddled,
    And if at times there'd also been 'high jinks',
    Even when there hadn't been some drinks,
    And if to recreate a painted kiss,
    The minister's intentions went amiss,
    And if some personal space had been invaded,
    While fears of this had also been downgraded,
Then some women, they did state, "That was Alex Salmond's
    habit!"
But Nicola Sturgeon, she insists she knew nothing then about it!

Nicola Sturgeon and Alex Salmond had some rather unusual
    conversations,
Concerning such events when there appeared some allegations.
(He could have been 'a better man', his lawyer in court admitted,
When Salmond was tried for sex assault, but found to be
    acquitted).

If some key discussion on this she'd 'forgotten',
And inquiry by officials turned out rotten,
Since with 'apparent bias' it was tainted,
For complainants and official were acquainted,
And if some forces 'dark' and 'sinister',
Were out to get the ex-first minister,
And if texts urged to 'pressurise' police,
Then "It's all her fault", said Salmond's devotees!
But Nicola Sturgeon, she maintains she didn't break the code
    with any sleaze!

Nicola Sturgeon and Alex Salmond no longer figure in the same
        party;
She leads the nation at the top; he's got a show on RT.
And each can use their platforms to display their gift of gab,
But their cybernat supporters think the other's just a scab.

    And if there is another referendum,
    Or even more, the famous neverendum,
    Whichever way events then do transpire,
    Each will doubtless wave their own saltire.
And everyone will say, there can be no concordat
Between Nicola Sturgeon and Alex Salmond - and some of the
    time they might leave it at that!

OH, JEREMY CORBYN

Old Jeremy Corbyn spent a long time,
    In fact, decades, defying his own party whip;
Was elected as leader and then he said, "I'm
    The boss now, so all must obey my new leadership."
"Oh, Jeremy Corbyn" was the refrain
    He heard chanted at Glasto and liked what he heard.
He said seats were too full when he travelled by train;
    And when hearing the anthem he'd not sing a word.
At the sound of him reading out questions that poured in
    When he stood in his place at prime minister's Qs,
Most MPs behind him thought: "Now, just whose
    Fault ... Can it be ... really! ... No! ... Yes! ...
        His tie
        Is awry!
The Tories are floundering, but oh what a mess,
We've landed ourselves with Jeremy Corbyn!"

Old Jeremy Corbyn bought smarter suits;
    Won votes when May showed herself wobbly and weak;
Had support from Momentum, they were in cahoots,
    But in polling his own personal ratings were bleak.
His fans liked to call him 'the absolute boy';
    They hoped he'd displace some conservative norms.
Yet if asked about Jews, then that him would annoy;
    So he'd talk about racism's 'all other forms'.
On Facebook he'd seen a caricatured drawing,
    Antisemitic, which he wrote to defend.
Those he'd upset then remarked: "In the end,
    Well ... Can it be ... really! ... No! ... Yes! ...
        His views
        Aren't for Jews!
This is an issue he tries not to address,
And the cause of our stress is Jeremy Corbyn!"

Old Jeremy Corbyn sang the Red Flag
  With gusto; his hero was A. Wedgwood Benn.
When Remain's chances of winning had started to sag,
  He scored the EU only seven from ten.
Recalling events he just said he was 'present',
  Did not 'get involved' (it helped avoid trouble).
His stance on Russian poison was much thought unpleasant;
  As polling day neared, Labour's problems did double.
He hoped in his heart for his legacy's glorying,
  But his aim to win power then came to naught;
As the voters of Britain said: "What a thought,
    Well ... Can he be ... really! ... No! ... NO! ...
      The red wall
      Is appalled!
While he's friend to the few, for many he's foe,
It's time to say bye to Jeremy Corbyn!"

DONALD J TRUMP'S LAST STAND

Trump, Donald J, was President, and number forty-five.
Indeed he often called himself the smartest man alive!
From morning up to evening he maintained a flow of tweets,
While munching through Doritos and McDonalds for his eats.

His manners and appearance did not calculate to cheer;
His hair was overcombed at front and sprayed down at the rear;
His face was coloured orange, all the way up to both eyes;
And if he had to make a speech HE UTTERED BLATANT LIES.

He tweeted at the media that they produce fake news;
He tweeted at Kim rocket man the button he could use;
He tweeted out an odd new word, it just said 'covfefe';
No one found out what that meant - still puzzles all, however.

And then on goods of foreign source new tariffs he had vowed;
For steel of Chinese origin no import was allowed.
Of Presidents, he told the world, I'm one that's done the most;
United Nations delegates laughed at this far-fetched boast.

The people of America were polarised on Trump;
Some wanted him to build a wall and also drain a swamp.
In 2020 foes did know they'd have another chance;
The Democrats picked SLEEPY JOE, their prospects to enhance.

As Covid hit, so many states allowed more votes by post;
Trump sought a way to block all that, in case it hurt him most.
His lawyer GIULIANI then was one of Trump's top fans,
But Rudy spent his time with fake reporters from the Stans.

So in his office, oval-shaped, the Donald lonely sat;
The justices might help him out if AMY CONEY sat.
He'd get her past the Congress first, so that's the plan, he thought;
If matters went from bad to worse, he then could go to court.

November 3rd, election day: and voters stood in queues
(In line, Americans would state); it was the point to choose
A President and join a camp for who would be the best -
Trumpists versus Bidenites, though some picked KANYE WEST.

The time had come to count the votes and find out who had won.
But at the start the Donald screamed "I know that I've been done!"
As several states seemed set to flip, it looked like Joe had scored.
Said Trump: "I can explain all that, it's just because of fraud!"

His lawyers said: "We need a place to tell the media
Our case, a nice hotel perhaps - not somewhere seedier."
And someone said, it's not clear who, "Oh, I know just the spot:
Four Seasons Total Landscaping, it's got a parking lot."

As Rudy lectured journalists, the networks made their call:
That Joe was top, and Kamala - the margin wasn't small.
The Trumpists didn't like the facts, they chanted 'Stop the Count!',
But evidence that Biden won continued still to mount.

Trump lost in court his claims of fraud, yet one idea he had:
A cunning plan to make a call to RAFFENSPERGER, Brad.
He asked the Georgia Secretary to find him extra votes -
Eleven thousand. Brad declined, instead he leaked the quotes.

By 306 to 232 the College said: "You're fired!"
Trump tweeted at his followers to protest: "Will be wild!"
The Capitol was stormed that day, a shameful act was tried.
But after all was said and done, Joe's win was certified.

So eighty million voters then had given Trump the snub;
He departed from the White House for his Mar-a-Lago club.
His daughter, that's IVANKA, yes, did meet him at the door -
Now she is planning how she'll run in 2024.

OF THE ANTI-SOCIAL BATTLE OF THE WOKES AND THE POPULISTS
Together with some Account of the Participation of the Remainers and the Leavers, and the Intervention of the Meek Centrist Dad

The Wokes and the Populists like to work through
On all forms of social repeating their view,
In case there is someone who's not sure it's true.
And Remainers and Leavers, though most people state
That contest is over and feelings abate,
Some still have preserved their deep urge to berate,
And they
    Tweet tweet tweet tweet
    Tweet tweet TWEET TWEET
Until you can see them all over the screen.

They sit at their keyboards and tip-tap away,
They like to spot memes they can use to inveigh,
They hope to go viral, if just for a day.
By fixing on themes that prompt anger and moans
The twittering foes target points to condemn
(And if parallel jibes can be made against them,
Living in glass houses doesn't stop throwing stones),
So they type out their rage at what led to their groans.
And then many others behaving like clones
Hear the notification and pick up their phones,
And they start to
    Retweet retweet retweet retweet
    Retweet retweet RETWEET RETWEET
Until you can see them all over your feed.

In this public arena they find plenty to argue,
Or for those who prefer it, to signal some virtue.
What should be done with a Union Jack?

Is microaggression a form of attack?
And are Meghan and Harry the couple to back?
What should one mean by 'woman' or 'mother'?
Should you stay in your lane or switch to another?
If trading goes wrong, is it Brexit to blame?
A building called Gladstone, does it need a new name?
Should a statue be toppled and put in the sea?
What's the full meaning of taking the knee?
Is Elgar good music to play at a prom?
Is it othering someone to ask where they're from?
Just what are the things that it's ok to say
Without being called out for going astray?
The culture war
Has battles galore,
With a

      Tweet tweet tweet tweet
      Tweet tweet TWEET TWEET
  Until you can see them all over the screen.

They must find the right hashtags and get them to trend.
If someone annoys them, they're quick to unfriend.
For certain opponents they try to cause trouble,
And win lots of likes in their own filter bubble;
When someone's a target then on they will pile
With hostile posts. But now once in a while
Another voice thought there was something to add
To ongoing debate - yes, the meek CENTRIST DAD,
With a tentative view. But experience showed
The result straight away was he got ratioed!
Then more of his thoughts left the warriors yawning,
The Wokes and the Populists simply ignored him.
So both fight each other to get their lines out,
Adding phrases to show there is nothing to doubt:

So here's your reminder you're wrong and I'm right.
Period. End of. That's the poem. Goodnight.

THE BRITISH VOTER

The British Voters are a Curious blend:
If faced with higher spending, then they'd rather lower tax;
But discussing public services, they'd rather have the spend!
They also state the planet mustn't heat up to the max,
But raising petrol prices is a plan that they would end!
So all this causes trouble for what government enacts.
Yes, the British Voters are a Curious blend -
   And it isn't easy to befriend them:
     For they will think
     And counter think,
       And so it can be tough to comprehend them!

The British Voters are a Curious lot:
Building homes across the land, they say that's badly needed;
Developments aren't welcome though, because they're such a blot!
Immigration's high, they say, and has to be impeded;
But they want essential workers who we've currently not got!
Yet they moan it isn't fair if the public's views aren't heeded!
Yes, the British Voters are a Curious lot -
   And it might seem right to reprehend them:
     For they will think
     And counter think,
       And so it can be tough to comprehend them!

The British Voters are a Curious sort:
They say a 'postcode lottery' is really quite malign;
But local choice is something that they're eager to support!
They say they cannot bear it when MPs just toe the line;
But disunited parties will do badly at the polls!
It's good if leaders listen, as they might change their mind
(So the public likes to say, when talking of such roles),
Yet too they're praised for principles when they stick firm behind!

Such dissonance is common, one shouldn't be surprised.
If the voters are against it, then they also could be for.
And if that's pointed out, they won't feel compromised,
As consistency's a burden which they're happy to ignore.
Yes, the British Voters are a Curious sort -
    And there are lots of ways to offend them:
        For they will think
        And counter think,
            And so it can be tough to comprehend them!

THE SONG OF THE JOURNALISTS

Journalists like to send a tweet,
Journalists want to have their say;
So Reshuffle time is hard to beat -
Journalists long for a Reshuffle day.

Journalists hope to get some leaks,
Journalists search for scoops, of course;
Journalists have their pet techniques,
So on lobby terms, that's a background source.
Journalists hope events turn up;
Journalists doorstep in a scrum;
They keep a tally, who's down or up,
And wait for the Reshuffle day to come.

Journalists lurk around the lobby,
Journalists listen in a huddle;
Journalists can be quite gobby,
Heaven forfend they get in a muddle.
And if the quotes are off the record,
That doesn't mean the story ends -
Journalists note them, not ignored;
Journalists use the quotes, from 'friends'.

Journalists tend to hunt in packs;
Journalists praise but then berate;
Journalists (or should I say 'hacks')
Were somehow termed the Fourth Estate.
Rumours and whispers are often their trade;
They talk to their contacts in search of the goss;
They write up the statements the rent-a-quotes made;
They put out their stories, exclusives if poss.

Journalists like to probe and ask,
Journalists spill the beans; and I'm
A hack as well, but with a new task:
Which is how to get these lines to rhyme.
Yet me and my fellows, our feelings excite,
On the best of all days, the one that we'd choose,
We are waiting and saving ourselves to be right,
On the Reshuffle day with the Reshuffle news.

THE AD-DRESSING OF VOTERS

If someone is a democrat,
Then my opinion now is that
To win they'll need to get some votes,
Since that is what the term connotes.
And gaining voters nowadays
Is all about a nifty phrase,
Which straight at once encapsulates,
And furthermore communicates,
The rights or wrongs of any plan
Promoted by the partisan.
And some are better, some are worse -
But all may be described in verse.
Thus for a slogan they can voice,
The parties have to make their choice.
It matters more than one iota,
So
      How would you ad-dress a voter?

First, here's a point we must proclaim:
THE VOTERS ARE NOT ALL THE SAME.

Now when you think of people voting
A target must be those ones floating.
And then you'll need a shorthand term
To tag the voters you might turn.
It's often based on travel mode:
'Mondeo man' became a code
Which then was quite analogous
To 'on the Clapham omnibus';
And 'white van man' - another one,
He's often said to read The Sun.
Then 'Worcester woman', 'Aldi mums',
(Across the pond, they're 'soccer moms')

And 'Holby City women' too
Are also groups of those to woo;
While 'pebbledash people' have a home
Where canvassers are keen to roam.

And so again we can exclaim:
THE VOTERS ARE NOT ALL THE SAME.

But once you've sorted out the quotas
Of your kinds of target voters,
You can use these slogan tips
For pledges said with 'Read my lips':
Now one much liked is 'Time for change',
And after that there is a range
Of terms oft used, a phrase or word -
You then select the ones preferred.
A Britain 'better', 'stronger', 'fairer',
We will 'build' through work 'together';
Then to 'the future' moving 'forwards',
'Hope' and 'challenge' are the buzzwords.
Alliteration also aids
By better breaching brains' blockades.

Yet other themes can find cut-through,
Like "For the many, not the few",
And "Labour isn't working" when
"The lady's not for turning" then.
"Build back better", "Yes we can",
"Our long-term economic plan".
And tough on crime, and on its cause,
Is still a way to get applause.
For all to be best understood -
They've never had it quite so good!
To try to set a narrative,
Indeed - there's no alternative!

Soundbites are a form of spinning,
Are you thinking what I'm thinking?!
So none of this is now a mystery,
Since we spot the hand of history!

To say all this, that's why I wrote a
Guide how to AD-DRESS A VOTER.

THE AIMS OF POLITICIANS

Political motives are matters of doubt,
    For often they're subject to all sorts of claims,
From 'principled stance' to simply 'a sell-out' -
    Yet those wanting to lead may have MULTIPLE AIMS.
To start there are aims that the cynics suggest,
    Such as power or status or utmost ambition
Or fame or importance - some self-centred quest,
    Which may be the plan of a keen politician.
There are worthier aims that you also might notice,
    Some for the leftists, some for the right,
Such as greater democracy, freedom or justice,
    And these are good purposes many would cite.
Some MPs seek a mission more specialised,
    A challenge distinctive, their own favourite cause;
They then run campaigning that's more personalised,
    Perhaps get the credit for changing some laws.
In petitions, debates and media releases,
    The issues involved can make quite a range,
From lack of support for our exports of cheeses,
    To parking machines which don't give back change.
But while backing the causes in which they believe,
    And opportunistically striving for power,
Why then do they have such aims to achieve?
    Time now for a quote from SCHOPENHAUER:
You can do as you will, but not will what you will.
    This notion for all is most surely the same -
Not just politicians, but the rest of us still
    May ponder and ponder the source of our aim,
        Such diversified, unified,
        (Herein now versified),
Proud and personified multiple Aims.

CAT LARRY INTRODUCES HIMSELF

I once was a stray who resided at Battersea,
  But now I exemplify social mobility.
I've got a big job and so I find latterly
  I mix with world leaders and British nobility.

I moult on PMs, leave them covered in hairs;
  The Cabinet Room's a nice spot for my naps;
I greet all the guests on their way up the stairs;
  I prowl Downing Street so the press can take snaps.

At first in my role I became a success,
  Hunting down rodents all over the house;
Yet now that I'm famous, I have to confess,
  I just can't be bothered to look for a mouse.

But if Palmerston visits my duty compels
  I keep the Foreign Office away from my patch,
So I screech and I screech with yet more decibels,
  And if that won't deter then I'm happy to scratch.

I purred for Obama, I kept Trump's car waiting,
  I fought off the threats from the dog-lover Carrie,
I show off myself to the journos spectating -
  The cat who is top is the cat who's called Larry.

NOTE

The poems here are presented in a different order to the comparable verses in *Old Possum's Book of Practical Cats*. This is how they correspond:

Boris: The Prime Minister ~ *Skimbleshanks: The Railway Cat*

The Keir Starmer Way ~ *The Old Gumbie Cat*

Dominic Cummings: The Strategy Man ~ *Macavity: The Mystery Cat*

Mr Rishi Sunak ~ *Mr Mistoffelees*

Gove: The Nightclub Man ~ *Gus: The Theatre Cat*

Jacob Rees-Mogg: Man About Town ~ *Bustopher Jones: The Cat About Town*

Alex Salmond and Nicola Sturgeon ~ *Mungojerrie and Rumpelteazer*

Oh, Jeremy Corbyn ~ *Old Deuteronomy*

Donald J Trump's Last Stand ~ *Growltiger's Last Stand*

The Wokes and the Populists ~ *The Pekes and the Pollicles*

The British Voter ~ *The Rum Tum Tugger*

The Song of the Journalists ~ *The Song of the Jellicles*

The Ad-dressing of Voters ~ *The Ad-dressing of Cats*

The Aims of Politicians ~ *The Naming of Cats*

Cat Larry Introduces Himself ~ *Cat Morgan Introduces Himself*

Printed in Great Britain
by Amazon

69671264R00026